NAME OF ARTIST

Contact: hey@happylifemedia.org

Join our newsletter! www.happylifemedia.org

Images from Vecteezy.com

Magic
unicorn

Unicorn

www.ingramcontent.com/pod-product-compliance
Lightning Source LLC
LaVergne TN
LVHW082258150826
845677LV00009B/1659
9798421075363